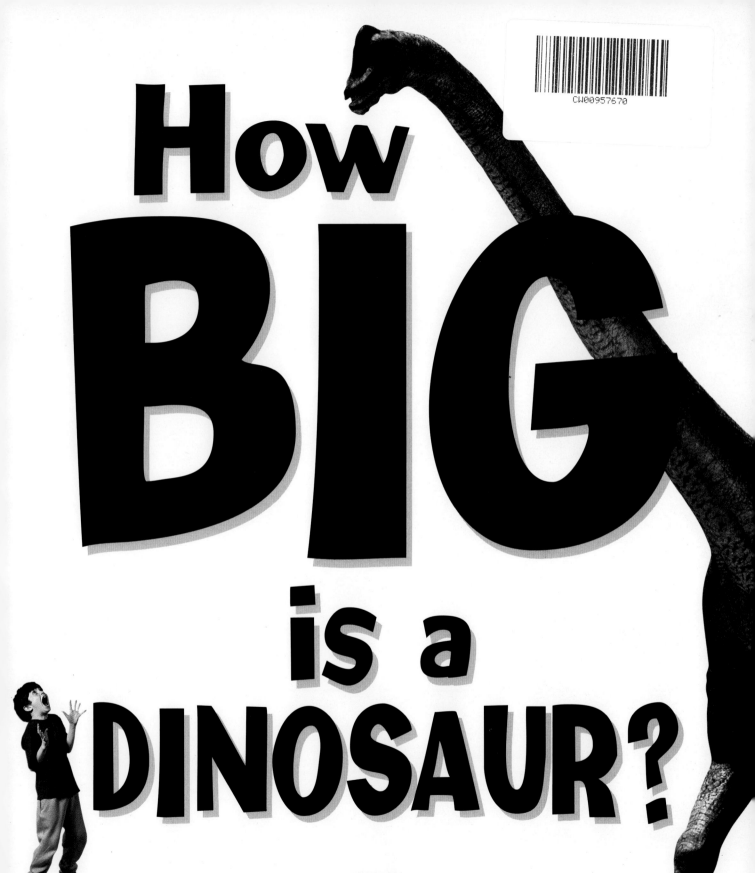

How BIG is a DINOSAUR?

BBC

What was a DINOSAUR?

Long, long ago, the world was a very different place. There were no people – instead, strange animals we call **dinosaurs** ruled over the planet.

Dinosaurs had tough, scaly waterproof skin – a bit like the crocodiles that live on Earth today.

The word 'dinosaur' means **terrible reptile**.

Dinosaurs have different names. **Stegosaurus** is one of the best-known dinosaurs.

Stegosaurus

How to say the words in **bold**:
Stegosaurus – say STEG-uh-SAW-rus

How big was a DINOSA

Dinosaurs came in all sorts of shapes and sizes. Some were no bigger than a chicken. Others would have towered over your house!

Scale markings on ruler: 0, 30, 20, 110, 1m, 90, 80, 70, 60, 50, 40, 30, 20

 How to say the words in bold:
Brachiosaurus –
say BRACK-ee-uh-SAW-rus
Diplodocus –
say Di-PLOD-uh-kus

UR?

Brachiosaurus was a huge dinosaur, weighing more than five elephants!

Brachiosaurus

The smallest dinosaurs of all, of course, were *baby dinosaurs!*

DiPPY

Diplodocus babies weren't very small – they'd weigh as much as a lorry by their first birthday!

5

What did DINO

There were only two things on a dinosaur menu – plants and raw meat!

Eustreptospondylus

Looking at a dinosaur's mouth can help tell you what it ate. **Eustreptospondylus** had sharp teeth and powerful jaws for eating meat.

SAURS eat?

Muttaburrasaurus had a beak-like mouth that helped it tug leaves from the trees for eating.

Muttaburrasaurus

 How to say the words in **bold**:
Muttaburrasaurus –
say MUT-uh-BUR-uh-SAW-rus
Eustreptospondylus–
say yoo-STREP-toh-spon-DIL-us

Could DINOSAURS fly?

Dinosaurs couldn't fly, but there were flying reptiles that shared their world. They were called **pterosaurs**.

How to say the words in **bold**:
Pterosaurs – say TEH-ruh-SAWs
Ornithocheirus – say or-NITH-oh-KYR-us

Some **pterosaurs** had a wing span as long as a bus!

vvvmm

Ornithocheirus

Ornithocheirus was a pterosaur. It had sharp teeth inside its beak. These helped it to eat the fish and squid it grabbed from the water.

Were DINOSAURS

Dwarf allosaur

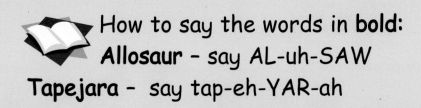 How to say the words in **bold**:
Allosaur – say AL-uh-SAW
Tapejara – say tap-eh-YAR-ah

different colours?

Tapejara was a pterosaur that used its brightly coloured crest to attract attention.

Tapejara

We don't know for sure, but we think dinosaurs were coloured to blend in with their surroundings. It made hunters like this **allosaur** hard to spot!

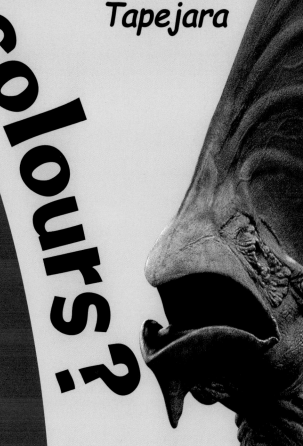

Were DINOSAUR-

friend

Iguanodon

How to say the words in **bold**:
Iguanodon – say i-GWAN-uh-don
Tyrannosaurus rex – say TIE-ran-uh-SAW-rus RECKS

Some dinosaurs liked company and moved in herds, like elephants do today. Meat-eating dinosaurs didn't make many friends – they were too busy trying to eat them!

y?

These **Iguanodon** moved around together for safety – if they travelled alone they became more at risk from hungry meat-eaters.

Tyrannosaurus rex was very dangerous, and always lived alone. It would attack almost any other dinosaur it met!

WANTED T-Rex

Could DINOSAURS Swim?

Liopleurodon was a massive sea-reptile. It could hold its breath for over an hour!

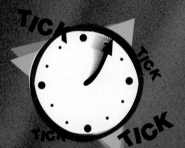

TICK TICK TICK TICK

Liopleurodon

Dinosaurs only lived on land, but other reptiles lived in the water – in many shapes and sizes!

How to say the words in **bold:**
Liopleurodon – say LYE-oh-PLUR-oh-don
Ophthalmosaurus – say op-THAL-mo-SAW-rus

Ophthalmosaurus

Ophthalmosaurus was probably the fastest prehistoric swimmer. It used its tail to push itself through the water.

Which was the DINOSAUR?

scariest

Tyrannosaurus rex needed to eat about 300 kilograms of meat every week – that's the weight of about four people!

It has to be...
Tyrannosaurus rex!

Its head was massive, its sharp, pointed teeth were the size of bananas... and we think it had a fantastic sense of smell!

Tyrannosaurus rex

 How to say the words in **bold**:
Tyrannosaurus rex
– say TIE-ran-uh-SAW-rus RECKS

Were DINOSAURS Fast or slow?

Diplodocus

Really large dinosaurs, like **Diplodocus**, probably moved quite slowly because they weighed so much.

Smaller dinosaurs were quite speedy – they needed to be, either to catch food or to run away!

Coelophysis

Coelophysis darted about quickly to attack its victims before they could bite back!

How to say the words in **bold**:
Diplodocus – say di-PLOH-duh-kus
Coelophysis – say SEE-luh-FYE-sis

What were DINOSAUR

Tyrannosaurus rex

babies like?

Dinosaurs hatched from eggs. Sometimes the eggs were hidden under the ground or in large nests.

This **Tyrannosaurus rex** is guarding her nest of eggs. Eggs were often eaten or destroyed by other dinosaurs.

How to say the words in **bold**:
Tyrannosaurus rex – say TIE-ran-uh-SAW-rus RECKS

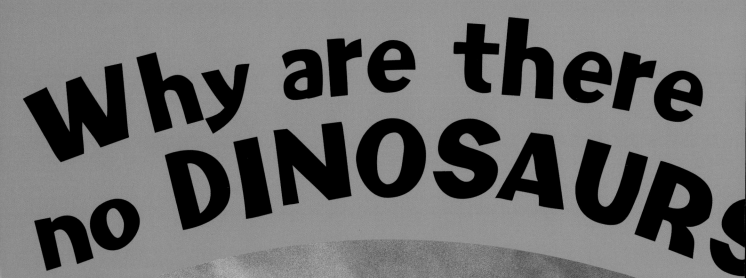

Why are there no DINOSAURS

Long ago, a big rock fell from the sky and crashed into our world. All the dinosaurs disappeared.

today?

We only know they were ever alive from the bones they left behind...

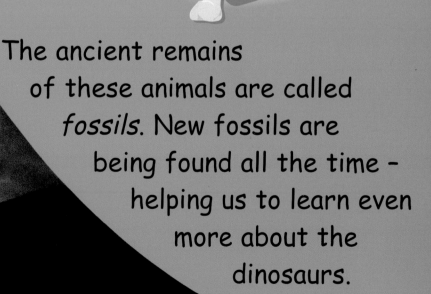

The ancient remains of these animals are called *fossils*. New fossils are being found all the time – helping us to learn even more about the dinosaurs.

The dinosaurs
lived over 100
million years
ago.

What sort of
animals do you
think we'll find
100 million years
from now?